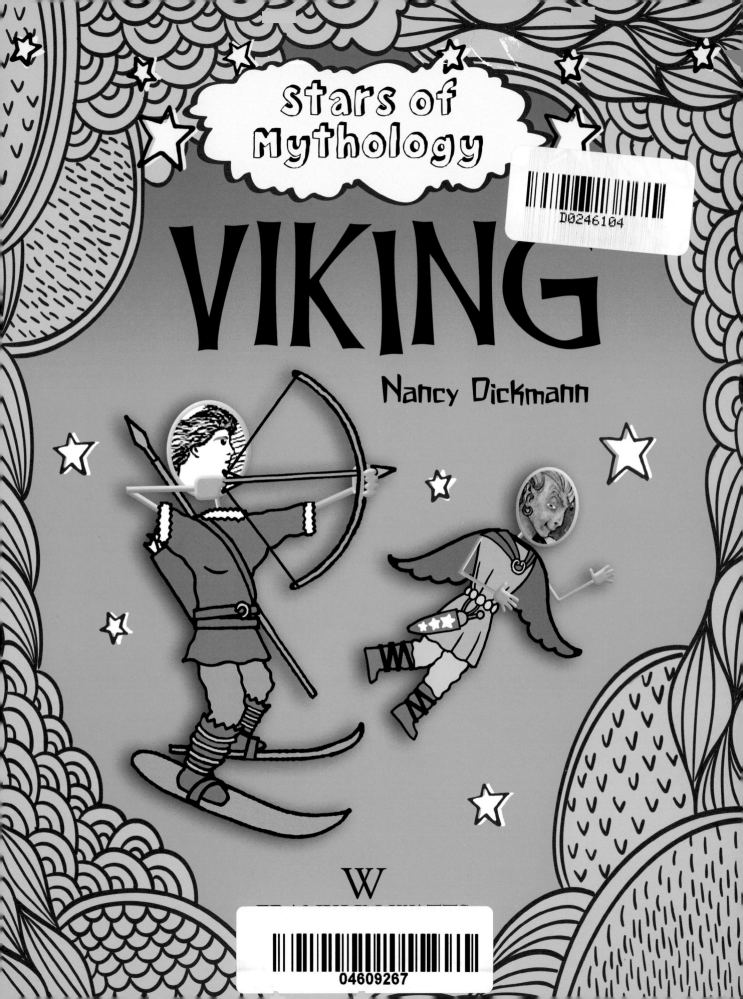

Stars of Mythology

VIKING

Nancy Dickmann

W

Franklin Watts

First published in Great Britain in 2017
by The Watts Publishing Group

Credits

Series editor: Sarah Peutrill
Series design and illustrations: Matt Lilly
Cover designer: Cathryn Gilbert
Picture researcher: Diana Morris

Pic credits: John Bauer/wikimedia commons: 1tr, 5b, 19cl, 29br.
Ivy Close Images/Alamy: 6cl, 8c, 9b, 12br, 20bl, 22c, 24cl, 25cl, 27, 28bl,
29bl, 29bc. Oleg Doroshin/Dreamstime: 4b. Mary Evans PL: 20c.http://
www.freepik.com">Designed by Freepik: front cover b/g. Andy Gehrig/
istockphoto: 15c.gevision/Shutterstock: 11 bg. Imagebroker/Alamy: 11c,
13t. Ying Feng Johansson/Dreamstime: 5t. Lebrecht: 18cl, 20, 21, 26,
28tr. H.L.M/ wikimedia commons: 1tl, 10c, 12t, 12bl.Oleksandr Mazur/
Shutterstock: 10b/g. Lu Mikhaylova/Shutterstock: 6-7 b/g. Kucher Serhil
/Shutterstock: 18 b/g. Grethe Ulgjell /Alamy: 23c, 24cr, 25cr. Manuel
Velasco/istockphoto: front cover cl & cr. Duncan Walker/istockphoto:
14c, 17cl. wikimedia commons: 7cr, 9t.

HB ISBN 978 1 4451 5188 5
PB ISBN 978 1 4451 5189 2

Printed in China

Franklin Watts
An imprint of
Hachette Children's Group
Part of The Watts Publishing Group
Carmelite House
50 Victoria Embankment
London EC4Y 0DZ

An Hachette UK Company
www.hachette.co.uk
www.franklinwatts.co.

Contents

Viking mythology

The Vikings were people from what is now Norway, Sweden and Denmark. From the 8th-11th centuries, they sailed off to trade and settle other areas. Wherever they went, they brought their language, Old Norse, and their beliefs with them.
In this way, Viking, or Norse, myths spread far and wide. Later Christianity gradually replaced Viking beliefs, and so their myths about gods, giants and great battles slowly faded from memory. Luckily, they were written down, so we can still read them today.

Yggdrasil and the nine worlds

Vikings believed in a universe centred around Yggdrasil, an enormous ash tree. In its branches were nine separate but interconnected worlds. One was Asgard, the realm of many of the gods, another was Midgard, where humans lived. These two were connected by a rainbow bridge called Bifrost. The other worlds were home to dead people (Niflheim – the underworld), giants (called jötuns), dwarves and elves.

The great war

According to the myths, long ago, there were two tribes of gods: the Æsir (say ee-sir) and the Vanir. A war broke out and lasted for many years. The gods fought each other with magic as well as weapons, but neither group could ever completely defeat the other. Eventually they called a truce and exchanged hostages. There was a period of peace, with the Æsir continuing to live in their home of Asgard, and the Vanir in Vanaheim.

Vikings carved dragons on their ships to make them seem extra-fierce.

The end of everything

The Vikings believed that the world of gods and humans would eventually end in an epic battle called Ragnarok, fought against the giants. There were many prophecies about who would live and die during this battle. At the end, the world would sink into the sea, but after a while it would be reborn, and some of the gods would return from the dead.

This carving showing a Norse story is almost 1,000 years old.

How do we know?

Most of what we know about Norse myths comes from Icelandic sagas, stories that were written down in Iceland between the 12th and the 14th centuries. There are also the Poetic Edda, collections of poems that tell stories of how the world came to be, as well as tales of the gods and their adventures.

Some Viking gods, such as Loki, could shape-shift into other forms.

Odin and Baugi

Read their story on pages 8–9.

Fact file: Odin

Odin was the chief of the Æsir gods. He and his brothers, Vili and Ve, were the sons of Bor and Bestla. The three brothers fought and killed the frost giant Ymir, and they used his body parts to create Midgard, our planet Earth.

Odin lived in Asgard with his wife, Frigg, and their children and other gods. He was constantly in search of wisdom and knowledge. He even gouged out one of his own eyes in exchange for a drink from a well with magical waters that gave him knowledge.

Odin in his own words:

The perks of being a god:
I can shape-shift into any form I want. Giants, animals — you never know what disguise might come in handy.

Check my ride:
My horse Sleipnir has eight legs, so it runs faster than any other horse.

It's all about the bling:
Once every nine days, my magical golden ring, Draupnir, makes eight copies of itself.

Fact file: Baugi

Baugi was one of the many giants in Norse mythology. After his parents were killed by a pair of dwarves, his brother Suttung caught the two dwarves and threatened to kill them. They offered Suttung the magical mead of poetry if he let them go. Anyone who drank it would become a wise poet.

Suttung tried a sip of the mead, but didn't give any to Baugi, who kept busy on his farm. Suttung hid the rest of the mead in the centre of a mountain, leaving his daughter Gunnlod to guard it.

Baugi in his own words:

My family:
My parents were hardly the sharpest knives in the drawer, letting themselves get killed by those dwarves. Suttung's not much cleverer – but don't tell him I said that!

Biggest annoyance:
Finding decent staff. My farm workers were so useless that they killed each other with their own scythes!

Life's so unfair:
Suttung thinks he's great because he's got the mead of poetry, but he's never given me – his own brother! – even a teeny-tiny sip.

A letter to Suttung

Dear Brother,

I hope you're well. How's the harvest going?

I have a bit of bad news to share with you. You know that mead you had hidden underneath the mountain? The stuff you would never let me touch? Well, about that...

A couple of weeks ago I had some trouble with my farm workers. They always liked to argue (who doesn't?) but this time it got completely out of hand. You'll never believe it, but all of them ended up dead! It was a bloodbath.

Well, as you can imagine, it left me in a bit of a bind. How was I going to get the harvest in? Then a giant called Bolverk turned up looking for work. He looked strong, and I was desperate. But he said he wanted a sip of your mead for his payment.

Now, I know that you don't let anyone touch your mead. So I didn't promise that I'd give it to him – I just said that I'd ask you. And there was no way that one man could do the work of all of my farm workers, so it wouldn't matter anyway.

But what can I say? I never expected him to be able to do it. He was out in the fields from dawn till dusk, doing the work of twenty men. He kept his side of the bargain, and then demanded that I help him get the mead.

Thirsty work!

Bolverk

You've got to believe that I never actually meant to help him steal it! I took him to the mountain where the mead was buried, and I drilled the tiniest of holes – way too small for a giant his size.

But quick as a flash, Bolverk turned into a snake and wriggled through the hole, then drank all the mead. Gunnlod was no use; she just let him drink it. I'm truly sorry, but he must have been a god, maybe even Odin, I tell you, and I don't like to think what he might have done to me if I hadn't helped him!

Looks like I owe you a barrel of mead next time you're up this way.

Your loving brother,

BAUGI
x

Yum, yum in my tum!

Skadi and Njord

Read their story on pages 12-13.

Thjazi, Skadi's father, tricked Loki (the trickster god – see page 19) into giving him the magical apples that kept the gods young and immortal. Without the apples, the gods started to age quickly. Loki was able to steal the apples back, and the other Æsir gods killed Thjazi in revenge.

Fact file: Skadi

Skadi was a young and beautiful giant who lived in the snowy kingdom of Thrymheim, high in the mountains. She was a skilled hunter and fighter, using skis to travel quickly around the cold lands of her home.

Skadi in her own words:

My family:
I'll admit that I'm a bit of a daddy's girl. I'll stick by my father no matter what!

Prized possession:
My skis.

Would like to meet:
My dream guy is young and handsome - preferably blonde - as well as kind and cheerful. If he turns out to be a god, then so much the better!

My happy place:
The cold's never bothered me, so I can't see myself living anywhere other than Thrymheim. Deep snow, biting winds and rocky peaks – what's not to like?

Fact file: Njord

Njord was one of the Vanir gods. After the long war between the Vanir and the Æsir ended in stalemate, he was one of the hostages chosen to go and live with the other side, to avoid further wars. So he and his son, Freyr, and his daughter, Freyja, settled in Asgard with the Æsir.

Njord was the god of the sea and was responsible for keeping sailors safe. Because the Vikings depended so much on sea travel, this made him a very important god! He was also a god of wealth and fertility.

Njord in his own words:

Life as a migrant:
It wasn't my choice to come and live with the Æsir, but they've treated me all right. I do sometimes miss my old home of Vanaheim, though.

My perfect day:
The sun is shining, the breeze is strong and I'm out on the water in a fast ship.

There's no place like home:
I live in a shipyard called Noatun. The calls of the seagulls, the rows of boats bobbing in the water – what's not to like?

Worst day ever

Dear Diary,

This has been my worst day ever. I was just finishing breakfast when the news came that the gods had killed Father. All for a few rubbish apples! I put on my armour, strapped on my skis and went to confront them.

I found them all having a feast in their hall, laughing and joking. But Odin listened to me – he isn't as fierce as everyone says. He offered me gold in compensation, but I was having none of it. A few lousy coins would never make up for my father's murder!

I was playing it cool, but from the moment I walked into the room I hadn't been able to take my eyes off Baldur. He was totally fit – the kind of man to keep a girl warm on a snowy day, if you know what I mean! So I told Odin that I would accept nothing less than having one of the gods for a husband. I didn't say which, but I knew who could take my mind off my grief.

Skadi

Baldur

Odin just laughed. "All right," he said, "but you'll have to make your choice by looking only at his feet!" He seemed to be finding the whole thing hilarious. I wasn't.

So one of the serving girls brought in long curtains, and the gods all hid behind them to take off their boots. One by one, pairs of bare feet appeared below the curtains. "There you go, Skadi," Odin giggled. "Choose your husband!"

Baldur had been the best-looking man in the room by a country mile, I reasoned, so he must have the best-looking feet as well, right? I looked down at the display.

There were hairy feet, smooth feet, calloused feet, feet with crooked toes - who knew that gods could be so imperfect? But then I spotted a pair of lovely ones: healthy golden skin, no callouses, strong ankles. That had to be him.

"This one," I told Odin. He raised an eyebrow, then pulled up the curtain to reveal ...

Njord!
The shaggy-haired sea god with sails for brains!

Agh, what have I done?
Like I said,

Worst. Day. Ever.

13

Tyr and Fenrir

Read their story on pages 16-17.

Tyr was a god of war, fearless and bold in battle. Loki once taunted him by saying that he could only stir people into fighting, but could never help them make peace. Viking warriors offered Tyr sacrifices of meat, blood or mead to ensure success in battle.

Fact file: Tyr

Alongside Thor and Odin, Tyr was one of the most powerful of the Æsir gods. In some versions of the myths he is the son of Odin, and his mother may have been a giant.

Tyr in his own words:

Views on war:
I say, the bloodier the better. As long as it's a fair fight, that is.

My lucky day:
It's got to be Tuesday. After all, it's named after me!

Least favourite animal:
I used to be a dog person, but not so much anymore. Give me a nice cuddly cat any day.

Biggest challenge:
Learning to use a sword with my left hand.

Fact file: Fenrir

The wolf **Fenrir** was the son of the trickster god Loki and the giant Angrboda. His two siblings were equally fearsome: the gigantic sea snake Jormungand, and Hel, the queen of the underworld.

There had been a prophecy that Fenrir would kill Odin at the final battle, Ragnarok. So the Æsir gods kept him with them in Asgard, to keep an eye on him. Only Tyr was brave enough to feed him, and as the years went by he grew bigger and bigger – and more fierce.

Fenrir in his own words:

My family:
My siblings and I may not be the cutest or gentlest creatures, but once Ragnarok comes, I wouldn't bet against us.

Don't talk to me about "walkies":
At first it was all right in Asgard. But now that I'm not a puppy anymore, the gods don't let me go anywhere by myself.

Favourite food:
I'll eat anything, and the bigger the portion, the better – I've got to bulk up for Ragnarok.

My catchphrase:
Grrrrrrrrrrrrr!

When good pets go bad

There are calls for an official inquiry after the notorious wolf Fenrir carried out yet another bloody attack.

Residents of Asgard are dealing with the fallout of the latest attempt to keep the gigantic wolf Fenrir under control. It was only a few months ago that Odin ordered that a solution be found to the wolf's rapidly-increasing size and strength.

"We knew we had to control him somehow," Thor told us. "So we told Fenrir it was just a game to test his strength. He'd let us tie him up with a chain, then we'd place bets on whether or not he'd be able to break free." But although the Æsir tried one chain after another, Fenrir broke through all of them.

The latest attack came when they tried a new form of restraint. We spoke to Skirnir, who commissioned the magical chain from the dwarves. "They made it out of things that can't exist, like the beard of a woman and the sound of a cat's footstep," he explained. "I know it sounds crazy, but if it's made out of impossible ingredients then it can do impossible things."

One of our sources was able to examine it, and reports that the chain looks and feels like a thin silk ribbon. But when it was brought to Asgard, Fenrir smelled a trap and refused to let the gods put it on him.

The goddess Frigg, who was at the scene, told us: "They could never get a chain on Fenrir against his will – he was just too strong." Fenrir finally agreed to let the gods put the chain on, but only if someone put their hand in his mouth to prove that it wasn't a trick. Tyr boldly stepped forward to volunteer, but when Fenrir realised that he was well and truly caught, he bit off Tyr's right hand.

"There was blood everywhere," Frigg told us. "It was awful, but Tyr has only himself to blame. Honestly, where were Health and Safety when they hatched that plan? I would have waited until Fenrir was asleep, or maybe put something in his food to knock him out. But nobody listens to me."

Grrrrr!

Snap!

Thor and Loki

Read their story on pages 20-21.

Fact file: Thor

One of the most famous and powerful of all the gods, **Thor** travelled through the sky in his chariot, hurling thunderbolts and striking fear into his enemies. He used his strength and skill to protect Asgard from giants and any other creatures who posed a threat.

Thor's main weapon was a hammer called Mjollnir. He also had a pair of iron gloves that helped him handle Mjollnir, and a magical belt that doubled his strength.

Thor in his own words:

All in the genes:
With a father like Odin and a giant for a mother, it's no wonder I ended up with more muscles than anyone else!

The perks of being a god:
No one has ever dared tease me about being ginger.

Don't knock it till you've tried it:
Some people use horses to pull their chariots, but I prefer goats.

Coolest kit:
Not only is my hammer, Mjollnir, incredibly powerful, but whenever I throw it, it flies back into my hand, ready for some more quality bashing.

Fact file: Loki

Loki was different from the other Æsir gods: he was a trickster who amused himself by causing mischief. He sometimes helped the gods, but just as often he taunted them and got them into scrapes. He was quick-witted and could come up with a plan to get himself out of any sort of sticky situation.

Loki became blood brothers with Odin, but his main concern was always his own self-preservation. He and Odin ended up fighting on opposite sides at Ragnarok, and neither survived.

Loki in his own words:

Biggest asset:
Most people would say it's my dashing good looks, but the truth? My brain. (Though it's not difficult to out-think a hammer-for-brains like Thor.)

What people think about me:
Sometimes I'm Mr Popular with the Æsir, and sometimes they treat me like their worst enemy. They need to learn how to take a joke!

Greatest skill:
I can shape-shift into anything you like. I've been a horse, a salmon, a seal and even an old woman.

Wedding mayhem

Freyr and Gerd

Read their story on pages 24-25.

Fact file: Freyr

Freyr and his twin sister, Freyja, were Vanir gods who were traded to the Æsir along with their father, Njord. A handsome, kind god of good harvests, wealth and peace, he proved so popular with his hosts that they gave him Aflheim, the land of the elves, to rule.

Freyr had several magical objects, including a golden boar called Gullinbursti that was big enough to ride like a horse, and a magical sword that could fight by itself. He also had a servant called Skirnir who helped him try to win over Gerd and get her to marry him.

Freyr in his own words:

Everybody loves me: Being a god of wealth, good weather and fertility makes me very popular.

Coolest kit: My magical ship, *Skidbladnir*, comes with its own wind, always blowing in the direction you want. And once I get where I'm going I can fold it up and carry it in my manbag!

Life is sweet: Aflheim is brilliant, but when I get tired of hanging out with the elves, I can visit Asgard, which is even better.

On my agenda: I'm ready to settle down with the right lady. I'm not picky, as long as she's beautiful.

Fact file: Gerd

Gerd and her father, Gymir, were both giants who lived in Jotunheim. Although humans and mortals loved Freyr, the giants were his enemies. The giants preferred the icy cold of their homeland to the sunshine and sweet breezes that Freyr brought.

Gerd was known for her great beauty, which is what attracted Freyr. She lived with her father in a great hall guarded by fierce dogs and surrounded by a ring of fire.

Gerd in her own words:

My family:
My dad is a bit over-protective. He doesn't often let me leave the hall, and the ring of fire around it tends to scare visitors away.

How to make me happy:
Don't bother promising me gold or jewels – my dad already has more than I could ever need.

Greatest fear:
I sometimes worry that I'll never find the right man to settle down with.

Playing hard to get

One of Asgard's most eligible bachelors is officially off the market. Tomorrow Freyr will finally marry Gerd, but how did it come about? Read on for an exclusive preview to the wedding of the year!

Freyr

Gerd

When Freyr spotted Gerd, it was love at first sight. It didn't matter that she was a giant, or that she lived in far-off Jotunheim. Once he saw her, he had to have her for his wife.

"He stopped eating; he stopped sleeping," the groom's father, Njord, told us. "No one liked the idea of a god marrying a giant, but he was determined. I'd never seen him like that before."

But Freyr didn't do his own wooing. "The giants hate Freyr, so there would have been trouble if he had suddenly turned up at Gerd's door," a source close to the god reported. "That's why he sent his servant Skirnir instead."

The loyal Skirnir was seen leaving Freyr's hall riding his master's horse, which can see in the dark, and carrying the magical sword that can fight by itself. "That's when I knew it was serious," our source said. "Freyr wouldn't hand over his most prized possessions without a good reason."

Freyr can offer you gold and these delicious magic apples?

Skirnir's meeting with Gerd took place behind closed doors, but we managed to find a dwarf who overheard part of their encounter. "He offered her gold, and the apples that keep the gods immortal, but she was having none of it," he said. "So Skirnir dropped the nice-guy act and threatened to kill her if she didn't agree. Gerd still said no. She knew that her father would tear the head off anyone who tried that."

So what made the lovely Gerd change her mind? She's refused to comment, but there are several theories circulating. Some think that Skirnir used magic, threatening to curse Gerd until she agreed. Others think that she was always willing to marry Freyr, but didn't want to come across as too eager.

The wedding is scheduled for midday, and rumour has it that the happy couple will make their home among the elves in Aflheim, after a honeymoon cruise on the magical ship *Skidbladnir*.

Frigg and Baldur

Read their story on pages 28–29.

Fact file: Frigg

Frigg was the wife of Odin, which made her one of the most important of the Æsir gods. She was the mother of Baldur and Hod. She was worshipped as a goddess of motherhood, love and marriage, as well as of crafts such as spinning and weaving.

Frigg was an expert at a type of magic called *seidr*, which involved seeing into the future and understanding people's destiny.

Frigg in her own words:

Home sweet home: My halls in the land of Fensalir may be in a swamp, but they're still pretty fab.

They don't call me queen for nothing: I'm the only god that Odin lets sit on his throne, Hlidskjalf. It's got an amazing view – you can see all of the cosmos from there!

It's all about the entourage: I've got a lot to manage, so I have eleven maidservants to help me.

Most precious possessions: My two boys, Baldur and Hod. (Especially Baldur, if I'm completely honest.)

Fact file: Baldur

Baldur was the son of Frigg and Odin, and he was known for being gentle and thoughtful as well as handsome and cheerful. He was so beloved that he was said to radiate light wherever he went. His hall, Breidablik, was one of the finest in all of Asgard, and no lies could pass through its walls.

The giant Skadi wanted to marry Baldur, but she was tricked into choosing the sea-god Njord instead. Baldur's wife was called Nanna. There was a prophecy that when Baldur died, his death would signal the beginning of Ragnarok.

Baldur in his own words:

My philosophy:
I'm a lover, not a fighter. Life is short, so why waste time squabbling?

Check my ride:
Some people say that my ship, *Hringhorni*, is the largest of all ships. It would take a giant to launch it.

Biggest fan:
My mother is just the absolute best. She would do anything for me.

Favourite sport:
Dodgeball. I'm the champ, and I don't even have to dodge!

A mother's love: Frigg's diary

13TH DAY OF SKERPLA✲:

Baldur came to me today to say he'd been having nightmares about his own death. What could this mean? I had a chat with Odin and he headed off on Sleipnir to consult a wise woman.

14TH DAY OF SKERPLA:

Bad news – Odin's back and the wise woman told him that Baldur's doomed. But there's got to be a way out of this. I mean, we're gods, right?

15TH DAY OF SKERPLA:

I've had a brilliant idea. Baldur can't die unless something kills him, so all I need to do is to make everything in the world promise not to hurt him. How hard can that be?

Promise?

Ha ha!

4TH DAY OF HAUSTMANADUR:

Ugh, I'm glad that's over. I've been flying through all the nine worlds for months, but I think I've done it! Every rock, every tree, every animal, every disease – all of them have promised not to hurt Baldur. Now I can rest easy.

11TH DAY OF GORMANUDUR:

Everyone's favourite new game is to throw things at Baldur. Nothing hurts him – everything just bounces off! It's good to have a bit of fun after all that worry.

2ND DAY OF YLIR:

My beloved boy is dead, and it's all my fault! Everyone was playing 'let's throw things at Baldur' again, and poor blind Hod was left out of the fun, as always. So Loki gave him an arrow made of mistletoe and helped him aim it. As soon as I saw what was in his hand I knew I had made a mistake: I never made the mistletoe swear the oath! The dart hit Baldur and he fell down dead – killed by his own brother.

3RD DAY OF YLIR:

My stepson Hermod is a good boy. He volunteered to go to the underworld and plead with Hel to release Baldur and send him back to us. She agreed, but only if everything in the world wept for Baldur.

20TH DAY OR YLIR:

We've been sending messages out all over the cosmos, telling everyone to shed a tear for my lovely boy. And everyone has – except for a vile old giant called Thokk. She refused, so Baldur is lost to us forever.

✿Skerpla, Haustmanadur, Gormanudur and Ylir were all the names of months in the old Norse calendar.

Glossary

Æsir one of the two tribes of gods in Norse mythology. Many of the most famous gods, including Odin, Thor and Loki, were Æsir.

Asgard one of the nine worlds in Viking mythology. Asgard was the home of the Æsir gods.

chariot a carriage with two wheels that is pulled by horses or other animals.

cosmos the universe, seen as an orderly system.

destiny the events that are going to happen to a particular person or thing in the future.

dwarf a creature in Norse mythology that lives in the underground world of Svartalfheim. Dwarves were famous for their metalwork skill.

giant in Norse myths, giants and giantesses have super-powers, including super-human strength, but they are not necessarily any taller than humans.

hall a large building with a single room, where people or gods lived and gathered for celebrations.

hostage a person held as security to make sure that someone else keeps their side of an agreement.

immortal living forever and never dying or decaying. The Norse gods and goddesses were somewhat immortal: they wouldn't die of old age, although they could be killed.

jötun one of a super-human race of powerful, destructive creatures most often translated into the word 'giant', see above.

mead an alcoholic drink made from fermented honey. In Norse myths, those who drank from the mead of poetry became wise poets.

Midgard one of the nine worlds of Norse mythology, where humans lived. It was connected to Asgard by the rainbow bridge Bifrost.

migrant someone who moves from one country to another in order to find better living conditions.

myth a traditional story that tries to explain why the world is the way that it is, or to recount legendary events.

Norse a name for the people of ancient or medieval Scandinavia (Norway, Sweden, Denmark, Iceland) as well the name of their language, Old Norse.

prophecy a prediction about something that is going to happen in the future.

Ragnarok the final battle between the Norse gods and the powers of evil.

sacrifice to give a gift to the gods, such as food or a slaughtered animal. Sometimes even people were offered as sacrifices.

scythe a farm tool, with a long handle and a curved metal blade, used to cut down crops.

thunderbolt an imaginary pointed missile that flies down to earth along with a lightning flash. The god Thor could hurl thunderbolts.

tribe families or groups of people who share beliefs, language and a way of life.

trickster a person who cheats or deceives people.

underworld in Norse myths, the place, called Hel or Niflheim, where the dead went to live. Viking warriors who died in battle went to another place called Valhalla.

Vanir one of the two tribes of gods in Norse mythology. The Vanir lived in Vanaheim.

Books

D'Aulaires' Book of Norse Myths, Ingri D'Aulaire,
NYRB Children's Collection

Illustrated Norse Myths, Alex Frith and Louis Stowell,
Usborne

Treasury of Norse Mythology, Donna Jo Napoli,
National Geographic

Everyday Life, Art and Culture (Discover the Vikings),
John C Miles, Franklin Watts

Websites

Go here to read and listen to more stories from Norse mythology:
www.storynory.com/category/myths/norse/

This website will tell you more about the Vikings and their beliefs:
www.bbc.co.uk/schools/primaryhistory/vikings/beliefs_and_stories/

Find out more about some of the Norse gods here:
http://quatr.us/germans/religion/

On this website you can learn about Viking life, as well as their gods:
www.dkfindout.com/uk/history/vikings/

Note to parents and teachers: Every effort has been made by the Publishers to ensure that these websites are suitable for children, that they are of the highest educational value, and that they contain no inappropriate or offensive material. However, because of the nature of the Internet, it is impossible to guarantee that the contents of these sites will not be altered. We strongly advise that Internet access is supervised by a responsible adult.

Index

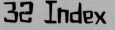